20 Reproducible Literature Circle Role Sheets
for Grades 1-3

Written by Christine Boardman Moen

Illustrated by Janet Armbrust

Teaching & Learning Company

1204 Buchanan St., P.O. Box 10
Carthage, IL 62321-0010

This book belongs to

_____

Dedication

This book is lovingly dedicated to my children, Alex and Ruth.

Special thanks to Judy Mitchell and Jill Eckhardt who encouraged me to write this book. Special thanks also to everyone at the Rockford Public Library for being so helpful– especially Andrew Finkbeiner and Carolyn A. Gray.

Cover by Janet Armbrust

Copyright © 2000, Christine Boardman Moen

ISBN No. 1-57310-219-9

Printing No. 987654321

Teaching & Learning Company
1204 Buchanan St., P.O. Box 10
Carthage, IL 62321-0010

TABLE OF CONTENTS

Dear Teacher or Parent,

If you're looking for a student-centered, literature-based activity that will help get your students excited about reading, then you're looking for literature circles. Simply put, literature circles are student-run book discussion groups. During each literature circle, students first respond individually to the literature they've read and then ask and answer questions and give ideas to explore the literature in more detail.

Literature circles can be a wonderful part of your reading program. And because there isn't one "right" way of conducting literature circles, you can decide what's right for you. An explanation of four types of literature circles is provided for you.

The overall literature circle approach described in this book utilizes student Response-Discussion sheets as well as student role sheets that students prepare prior to going to their discussion group. Each type of sheet allows students to respond individually to the literature as well as prepare for discussion. When it's time for their literature circle, students take their completed sheets to their discussion groups.

In addition to the 20 reproducible Response-Discussion sheets and student role sheets, this book contains text sets with over 175 book titles that will help your students enjoy a variety of literature circles. Moreover, teacher tips and assessment pages will help your literature circles run smoothly.

So, read the introductory material; gather your books and get ready for your students to enjoy reading, responding to and discussing books!

Happy, happy teaching!

Christine

Christine Boardman Moen

WHAT ARE LITERATURE CIRCLES?

Simply put, literature circles are student-run book discussion groups. Although there isn't one "right" way of doing literature circles, at the primary grade level most literature circles have the following characteristics:

Student groups usually consist of two to five students. Groups consisting of three to four students generally work best.

Student groups are determined by student book choice. Students select their own books from the text set established by the teacher. A text set is a group of different books related to a theme, author, genre or some other connecting element. (Lists of text sets along with brief teacher tips are provided later in this book.)

Text sets may include books which students are not able to read independently. The teacher, parents or older students may read the books aloud to students. In addition, students may "buddy read" or listen to the book on tape.

Student groups are not permanent. Groups change after the completion of the literature circle.

At the primary level, students usually meet once to discuss their book. Depending upon the book choice and number of students per group, literature circle response-discussion time usually lasts from 20 to 45 minutes.

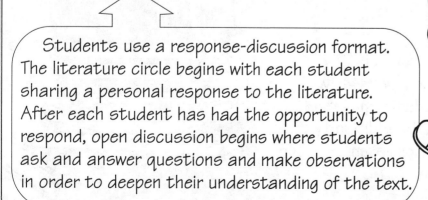

Students use a response-discussion format. The literature circle begins with each student sharing a personal response to the literature. After each student has had the opportunity to respond, open discussion begins where students ask and answer questions and make observations in order to deepen their understanding of the text.

Students in grade 3 who read longer chapter books can use the response-discussion format, or they may wish to choose between several student roles to use as discussion prompts. (How to use student roles is discussed in the How Do Literature Circles Work? [pages 14-19] portion of this introduction.)

The teacher's role is one of facilitator. In other words, the teacher is not a member of the discussion group although she or he may step in to ask a question, help solve a dispute or model a social cooperative learning skill such as using quiet voices.

Literature circles can be assessed using the Teacher Observation Checklist, the Student Self-Evaluation Sheet and the Group Evaluation Sheet in this book or through your own check-lists, rubrics or anecdotal records.

WHY USE LITERATURE CIRCLES?

At the primary grade level, literature circles should be one component of an over-all reading program. Literature circles add another dimension to students' literacy experiences and help boost their enthusiasm for reading while nurturing a sense of community. More specific reasons for providing students with literature circle opportunities include the following:

Literature Circles . . .

- **allow all students to succeed regardless of reading level or ability.**

  Student choice is an important component of literature circles. Although at times the entire class may be reading the same text, usually literature circles are based on text sets which include a variety of books of varying degrees of difficulty but ones which are related to one another in some way.

- **utilize cooperative learning strategies and social cooperative learning skills.**

  Literature circles capitalize on the positive interdependence and individual accountability aspects that are hallmarks of cooperative learning. With literature circles, students work within a group setting with the common goal of sharing ideas about the same book or same type of book. In order to achieve this common goal, each student must fulfill the responsibilities of his or her individual Response-Discussion sheet. At the same time, literature circles encourage the reinforcement of social cooperative learning skills such as using quiet voices, looking at one another while speaking and listening, and not interrupting while others are speaking.

Literature Circles . . .

- **encourage students to be positive members of a literate classroom community.**

  Surrounded by books and book discussions, students can't help but be drawn into a spirited community that respects readers and writers. Moreover, since students choose their own books and direct their own discussions, they become active learners who tend to assume responsible ownership of their learning.

- **capitalize on how students personally respond to literature.**

  Each literature circle Response-Discussion sheet allows students to respond to the literature in a way only they can. Each response portion of the sheet allows students to respond to the literature using their own unique point of reference and prior knowledge. At the same time, the discussion portion of the sheet encourages students to explore the text more deeply by raising questions and making observations.

- **encourage multiple readings of the text.**

  Because students use the text of their books to ask and answer questions about everything from interesting words to character traits, students read and reread the text to clarify their questions and support their answers.

WHAT ARE TEXT SETS?

A text set is a group of different books related to one another in some way. They may be related by theme, author, genre or any other connecting element you consider to be significant. For example, the different books in a text set may be related to one another because each deals with the issue of extended families. At the same time, books in another text set may be related to one another simply because they have bears as main characters.

The text sets provided in this book represent a very broad range of titles and topics. Students in grades 1-3 should be able to read independently some of the titles on the lists. However, since the goal of literature circles is to get students to make connections to the literature and discuss it in-depth, many books on the list may have to be read aloud to students since many books with very limited text may not be suitable for in-depth student discussion.

Since literature circles represent only one component of the reading-literature program, the listed text sets do not attempt to coordinate popular primary grade themes such as family, nature, friends and community. Instead, the text sets in this book are classified using broad cross-curricular categories such as multicultural fairy tales, historical fiction, stories based on math concepts and books representing different artistic styles. By creating text sets based on broad cross-curricular categories, the lists represent books that vary in length and degree of difficulty and include "tried-and-true" titles as well as newer titles you may wish to add to your school or classroom library.

And what about books in your classroom library? They can be a wonderful source of books for literature circles not only because they can be coordinated with classroom themes but also because they encourage independent reading. After all, beginning readers need lots of experiences with simple yet imaginative alphabet books such as *On Market Street* (Greenwillow, 1981) and counting books such as Pat Hutchin's *One Hunter* (William Morrow, 1986). In addition, beginning readers need to fall in love with pattern books such as *Brown Bear, Brown Bear What Do You See?* (Henry

Holt, 1967) and wonderful books of easy-to-read poems. At the same time, beginning readers need to be surrounded with reading chart books, bulletin boards and classroom walls filled with words and pictures.

Just as a plane takes off in flight, so, too, does the beginning reader advance from *Each Peach, Pear Plum* (Viking, 1986) to *Frog and Toad Are Friends* (HarperCollins, 1979) to *The Snowy Day* (Viking, 1981) and *Dr. De Soto* (Farrar Straus Giroux, 1982). At last, the student lifts off into fluent reading with first novels. Thus, getting students off the ground and into flight is the purpose of the primary grade classroom library which is critical to any reading program and which can be used as a source of books for literature circles.

How Are Text Sets Created?

One way of creating a text set using your classroom library is to choose a theme, author, genre or connecting element and explore your library for multiple copies of appropriate books. For example, bears are often featured in picture books and books for beginning readers. To accommodate a wide variety of reading abilities and interests in your classroom, you may want to choose several titles such as the following:

Mooncake
Frank Asch
Prentice-Hall, 1983

Clap Your Hands
Lorinda Bryan Cauley
Scholastic, 1992

Bears on Wheels
Stan and Jan Berenstain
Random House, 1969

Brown Bear, Brown Bear, What Do You See?
Bill Martin, Jr.
Henry Holt, 1967

Bears in Pairs
Niki Yektai
Macmillan, 1987

The Valentine Bears
Eve Bunting
Clarion, 1983

If you have two, three, four or five copies of a specific title, you have enough for one literature circle group. If you can manage to get multiple copies of several titles, you can offer students a choice of books. Thus, the two to five students who read *Bears in Pairs* form a literature circle while the students who read *Bears on Wheels* form another circle and so forth.

Each of the text sets provided in this book lists 12 titles. Each list has been compiled specifically to represent a broad range of text lengths, cross-curricular areas, representative student populations and student interest areas. You are encouraged to use the books which best suit you and your students.

Additional sources which can provide you with useful book lists and information about literature and literature circles include the following:

BOOKS

Learning to Read with Picture Books by Jill Bennett (The Thimble Press, 1991)

Better Books! Better Readers! How to Choose, Use and Level Books for Children in the Primary Grades by Linda Hart-Hewins and Jan Wells (Stenhouse Publishers, 1999)

Literature Circles and Response edited by Bonnie Campbell Hill, Nancy J. Johnson and Katherine L. Schlick Noe (Christopher Gordon Publishers, 1995)

MAGAZINES

Book Links (http://www.ala.org/BookLinks)

The Horn Book Magazine (http://www.hbook.com)

The Reading Teacher (http://www.reading.org)

LIBRARIES

Libraries often offer book services to teachers which include supplying multiple copies of books. At the very least, libraries offer wonderful published lists of award-winning books as well as lists of "best books" created by students.

INTERNET

A good source for lists of children's books is the internet. Some address are listed below. You may use any search engine and type in "children's literature."

Children's Literature
http://www.ala.org/parentspage/greatsites/amazing/html

Children's Literature
http://www.childrenslit.com/

The Children's Literature Web Guide
http://www.acs.ucalgary.ca/~dkbrown/index.html

Children's Literature: Web Sites
http://www.lib.utexas.edu/Libs/Pcl/child/sites.html

HarperCollins: The Big Busy House
http://www.harperchildrens.com/index.htm

How Do Literature Circles Work?

Because there isn't one "right" way to do literature circles, teachers are encouraged to adapt the procedures described below to their own classrooms.

Procedure 1: Same Group Reads Same Title

Using Procedure 1, the teacher selects titles for a text set and has multiple copies of each title.

1. The teacher introduces the theme, genre, author or connecting element by reading aloud a core book to the entire class. This book may or may not come from the text set.

2. After reading the book, the teacher models responses to the literature and how to develop questions for discussion.

Using an overhead transparency of the Response-Discussion sheet provided with the text set, the teacher creates his or her response in the response portion of the sheet. While doing so, the teacher explains aloud what his or her response is and why she or he is responding in this way.

Using sticky notes or a lined bookmark card, the teacher searches the book and tags pages or jots notes on the card corresponding with any illustrations or passages that help explain or illuminate his or her response.

Next, the teacher models how to develop good discussion questions by first asking students what questions they might ask. Again, the teacher tags pages or jots notes on the bookmark card. The teacher also writes the question on the discussion portion of the Response-Discussion sheet and notes the page or some type of picture reminder in the space provided. The questions should be open-ended. Some examples may include the following:

What did you notice about . . . ?
Who is telling the story and how do you know this?
What other book does this remind you of? Why?
How did this story make you feel? Why?
What did you think about the illustrations? Why?
Would you change any part of the story? What? Why?
If you could ask the author one question, what would it be? Why?
Do the characters change in the story? How? If not, why not?

Of course, for beginning writers, a sticky note on a page and the word *duck* with a question mark behind it on the Response-Discussion sheet may be enough of a memory jolt to remind the student of his or her intended question.

3. After the modeling session, the teacher introduces each of the text set titles by briefly describing each one. Students get a few minutes to look at each book before choosing which one they'd like to read.

4. Students choose their book. This can happen in a variety of ways.

- Books and sign-up sheets can be put on a table and students can take turns signing up for their first, second and third choices.

   Note: The teacher must decide the number of titles to use and the number of students she or he wants in each circle. These factors will determine how many different literature circles there will be. Thus, students who sign up for book "A" will form one circle; students who sign up for book "B" form another and so forth.

- Students can write their names on a ballot listing their first, second or third choices.

- Names can be drawn at random and students can go forward and choose their book.

Regardless of the system the teacher chooses to use, it's important to keep track of which students do not get their first or second choices and allow them to choose their books first for the next round of literature circles.

5. Once groups are established, students read their book or have the book read aloud to them. The teacher may go to each circle and read the book aloud, parent helpers may assist, upper-grade children may be invited to visit the classroom and read, the group can listen to the book on tape in the listening center or the book can be sent home for parents to read aloud. Students who are able to read their books should either "buddy read" or sit in their circle and take turns reading aloud. (Students usually take turns with each one reading a double page spread.)

6. If possible, students should take their books home so they can read them several more times. (If the teacher is aware that the student may not have the support at home to have the book reread, he or she should enlist the aid of parent helpers and upper-grade students to read the book to the student one more time before the literature circle meets.)

7. During classtime, students prepare for their literature circle by completing their Response-Discussion sheets and also tagging pages or jotting notes on their bookmark cards. The teacher circulates the room to offer assistance and encouragement.

8. Before students gather in their circles, the teacher reminds students of some important social cooperative learning skills such as the following:

   - Use quiet "inside" voices.
   - Encourage everyone to participate.
   - No put-downs allowed.
   - Look at one another while speaking and listening.

9. The teacher appoints a Discussion Director for each group who leads the group to its designated discussion area. (Students should have their books and completed Response-Discussion sheet with them.) The Discussion Director shares his or her response first. Once each student has had an opportunity to share his or her response, the Discussion Director begins the discussion portion of the circle by asking one of his or her questions or by making an observation.

Note: After students become comfortable with literature circles, the response-discussion overlaps and becomes integrated. This is acceptable and desirable since you want students to have a natural discussion about the book.

10. During the first few times students engage in literature circles, the teacher may want to circulate through the room listening to the discussion, posing a question if a group seems "stuck" and helping students resolve any problems. At first, students may need reminders to use the text to ask and answer questions. Also, the teacher may need to demonstrate how to ask follow-up questions during discussion.

11. After the first literature circle, the teacher conducts a "debriefing" session with the entire class pointing out positive things that happened and demonstrating alternatives.

12. Books and Response-Discussion sheets are collected. The teacher reviews the Response-Discussion sheets, which can be placed in student folders or returned to students.

13. Before the next literature circle, the teacher makes overheads of the Teacher Observation Checklist, the Student Self-Evaluation Sheet and the Group Evaluation Sheet and explains how they can be used to improve the literature circles.

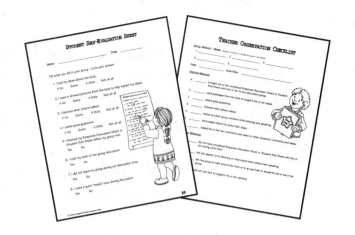

14. During the next round of literature circles, the teacher may wish to stay with one group and evaluate it using the Teacher Observation Checklist. When the students have completed their group discussion, each is given a Student Self-Evaluation Sheet to complete. Students return the evaluation along with their Response-Discussion sheet to the teacher for review. Once again, both sheets can be placed in student folders or returned to the students.

Procedure 2: Same Group Reads Different Titles

Using Procedure 2, students gather in literature circles for discussion, but each student may go to the circle with a different book from the text set. For Procedure 2, the text set includes an extensive list of titles related to one another either by author, genre, theme or other connecting element. The text set "Letters for Learners: ABC Books That Entertain and Teach" is an example of a text set which can be used for literature circles using Procedure 2.

Implementing the "Same Group Reads Different Titles" type of literature circle is the same as the previously described literature circle with a few exceptions. First, students should be encouraged to not only suggest types of text sets but also the titles to be included in the sets. Secondly, you will have to decide how to select students for each group since a single book selection will no longer determine group membership. One way to assign group members is to group students based upon Howard Gardner's Theory of Multiple Intelligences. An explanation of the theory and a group planning sheet appear at the end of these introductory pages.

The "Same Group Reads Different Titles" type of literature circle lends itself to discussion that focuses a great deal on comparing and contrasting. This type of circle also encourages students to read additional books on their own from the text set since students have had encouraging exposure to a variety of books during their literature circle time.

Procedure 3: Same Group Reads Two Different Titles

There may be times when you want students in the same group to discuss two different books that are related to each other in some way. For example, perhaps you'd like students to discuss books in which unusual things happen. You may want to choose Lawrence David's *Beetle Boy* (Doubleday, 1999) and Merrill Markoe's *The Day My Dogs Became Guys* (Viking, 1999). In the first story, the main character wakes up and discovers he's turned into a beetle. In the second story, the main character's three dogs turn into people for a day.

The procedure for introducing the text set and grouping students into literature circles is the same as in Procedure 1. There are many ways students can read the two different books. Groups of three students can take turns being the person in the middle who reads. Groups of four can "buddy read" each book, or the teacher can read one of the books aloud while each literature circle gets a different book with the same type of theme to use as comparison.

The text set "Alike but Different: Multicultural Cinderella Stories" especially lends itself to Procedure 3.

Procedure 4: Same Group, Same Title but Different Roles

Procedure 4 introduces different student roles to the literature circle process. Usually, student roles work best at the primary level after students have become very comfortable with literature circles and are able to read beginning novels such as those listed in the "Sensational Series: Book Series Too Good to Miss!" text set.

Since students should already be comfortable with the literature circle format, choosing books, and responding to and discussing books, the most significant addition to the overall process is the teacher introducing and modeling the different roles.

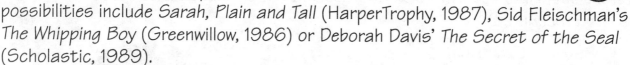

To prepare for the modeling session, select a book you can read aloud to the students over a two- to three-day period. Some possibilities include *Sarah, Plain and Tall* (HarperTrophy, 1987), Sid Fleischman's *The Whipping Boy* (Greenwillow, 1986) or Deborah Davis' *The Secret of the Seal* (Scholastic, 1989).

It may be easier for students if you introduce the Character Sketcher, Scene Setter and Dialogue Describer the first day. On the second day, students can be introduced to the Have-in-Common Connector, Decision Director and Wordsmith, leaving the Plot Person for the third and final day.

The steps in the modeling session, include the following:

1. The teacher explains that during this literature circle, students will choose from a text set, form groups based on their book selection and complete different student roles to take to their groups as discussion prompts.

2. The teacher introduces the Character Sketcher, Scene Setter and Dialogue Describer by showing the students overheads of the role sheets and providing each student with a copy of each role. The teacher explains the purpose of each role and directs the students to listen during the oral reading for ideas they can use to complete the role sheets.

3. The teacher reads the novel aloud, stopping after each chapter or whenever there is a natural break in the story. During each break, the teacher asks for suggestions for completing the roles. The teacher writes the suggestions on the overheads while the students write them on their sheets. As students make suggestions for role completion, they must use the text to support their ideas. Consequently, you may wish to tag those pages with sticky notes to demonstrate how students can use the notes to help them complete their role sheets after their initial reading.

4. On the board the teacher writes any questions the students pose about the text during the role completion session. This helps reinforce the idea that the role sheets are discussion prompts that serve to help overlap and integrate the discussion.

5. The next day, the teacher introduces the Have-in-Common Connector, Decision Director and Wordsmith roles and follows the same procedures as described previously.

6. On the third day, the teacher finishes reading the book aloud and introduces the Plot Person role and answers any questions about the various roles.

7. The next step is to introduce the books in the text set and to allow students to choose their books. Once groups have been decided, the students gather and decide which roles they'd like to complete. Encourage group members to choose a variety of roles, but don't be concerned if two students in the same group choose the same role. If groups seem to concentrate on one or two roles, you may have to assign different roles or draw role names at random.

8. As with previous literature circles, students read the entire book, complete their roles and meet once for discussion.

9. Use the information you gather from the Teacher Observation Checklist, the Student Self-Evaluation Sheet and the Group Evaluation Sheet to help students improve their discussions.

What Problems May Arise and How Do I Solve Them?

Problems that may occur usually involve absent students, uncooperative students and problems arising as a result of poor room arrangement. First, since primary grade literature circles usually meet only once, having an absent group member is significant. It's best to reschedule a group's literature circle rather than to proceed without one of its members.

In addition, to help with classroom management and to help students with their own time-management skills, it's best to hold literature circles on the same day each week. That way students will come to anticipate as well as expect literature circles on a specific day. At the same time, you should schedule make-up circles on another specific day. Using a predictable literature circle schedule helps students be prepared.

Another problem that may occur is getting an uncooperative student to be cooperative. A student who is uncooperative can be partnered with another student who is willing to work with him or her or can be put into a group comprised of students with whom the student wants to work and who are willing to work with the student. Each time the pair or group meets to discuss a book, you should review a list of acceptable and unacceptable behaviors.

Finally, don't let student groups disintegrate into chaos because of poor room arrangement. Group members should be "eye-to-eye and knee-to-knee" whether they're sitting on the floor, sitting around a table or sitting in a grouping of desks. Additionally, groups should be separated so they do not disturb one another and you have a clear walking path to each group.

How Do I Plan Groups Based on Multiple Intelligences?

If you decide to use Procedure 2 where each student in the same literature circle reads a different book, you may want to assign group members based on Howard Gardner's Theory of Multiple Intelligences which he first explained in his book *Frames of Mind: The Theory of Multiple Intelligences* (Basic Books, 1983). Simply put, the Theory of Multiple Intelligences is based on the idea that although every person is a blending of all of the many intelligences, each of us has a stronger inclination toward the way we receive, store and process information. In other words, one or more "intelligences" dominate our learning style making us better at some things than others.

The eight multiple intelligences are briefly described below and a general description of students who may demonstrate each intelligence area is provided. Student descriptions come from information printed in Nancy Boyles' *The Learning Differences Sourcebook* (Lowell House, 1997).

A Student Group Planning Sheet based on the intelligences appears on page 27.

Note: Using the Student Group Planning Sheet is in no way a scientific attempt to label students according to intelligences. It's merely a planning sheet to help create student groups.

Verbal-Linguistic Intelligence
These students like to read, write and tell stories. They enjoy word games, jokes and puns. They also like to learn new words, speak in public and read poetry.

Logical-Mathematical Intelligence
These students like to work with numbers, analyze situations and use reasoning skills. They understand abstract patterns and like to have clear "right" or "wrong" answers.

Visual-Spatial Intelligence
These students like to look at maps, draw, paint and solve puzzles. They like to take things apart and put them back together and create three-dimensional objects.

Body-Kinesthetic Intelligence
These students like to play sports, use body language, do crafts and be physically active. They like to dance, act, mime and create mechanical projects.

Musical-Rhythmic Intelligence
These students like to listen to and play music. They enjoy singing, humming and creating tunes. They are aware of patterns in rhythm, pitch and timbre.

Interpersonal Intelligence
These students like to build consensus with others and enjoy working as team members. They like to lead, share and mediate as well as brainstorm ideas to get others' feedback.

Naturalist Intelligence
These students enjoy being outdoors, observing plants, collecting rocks and listening to the sounds of nature. They enjoy working with plants, animals and the environment.

Intrapersonal Intelligence
These students know their own strengths and weaknesses. They like to set their own learning goals. They learn by listening and observing others.

STUDENT GROUP PLANNING SHEET

Name	Verbal	Math	Visual	Body	Music	Inter	Nature	Intra
1.								
2.								
3.								
4.								
5.								
6.								
7.								
8.								
9.								
10.								
11.								
12.								
13.								
14.								
15.								
16.								
17.								
18.								
19.								
20.								
21.								
22.								
23.								
24.								
25.								
26.								
27.								
28.								
29.								
30.								

	Group 1	Group 2	Group 3	Group 4	Group 5	Group 6
1.						
2.						
3.						
4.						
5.						

Teacher Observation Checklist

Group Members' Names Student numbers or initials are used in the blanks.

1. _____ 2. _____ 3. _____

4. _____ 5. _____

Date: _____ **Book Title:** _____

Positive Behaviors

a. _____ brought his or her completed Response-Discussion Sheet or Student Role Sheet with him or her to the discussion group.

b. _____ used passages from the book to support his or her ideas.

c. _____ asked good questions.

d. _____ listened while others talked.

e. _____ looked at other group members while listening and speaking.

f. _____ encouraged others to share their ideas.

g. _____ added his or her own comments and ideas to other students' comments and ideas.

Negative Behaviors

a. _____ did not have completed Response-Discussion Sheet or Student Role Sheet with him or her during circle time.

b. _____ did not appear to be listening or interrupted when others were speaking.

c. _____ left the group to walk around the room or to go and talk to students not in his or her group.

d. _____ did not use text to support his or her opinions.

Comments: _____

_____

_____

_____

_____

STUDENT SELF-EVALUATION SHEET

Name: _____ **Date:** _____

Tell what you did in your group. Circle your answer.

1. I told my ideas about the book.

   A lot   Some   A little   Not at all

2. I read or showed pictures from the book to help explain my ideas.

   A lot   Some   A little   Not at all

3. I listened when others talked.

   A lot   Some   A little   Not at all

4. I asked good questions.

   A lot   Some   A little   Not at all

5. I finished my Response-Discussion Sheet or Student Role Sheet before my group met.

   Yes   No

6. I took my book to the group discussion.

   Yes   No

7. I did not leave my group during our discussion time.

   Yes   No

8. I used a quiet "inside" voice during discussion.

   Yes   No

GROUP EVALUATION SHEET

1. _____ 2. _____ 3. _____ 4. _____

Follow the numbered directions to tell how the group did during its literature circle discussion.

1. The **first** student to answer the questions begins at the **bottom** of the page.
2. Put a number in the blank in front of each sentence. Use the scale below.
3. After you have answered the questions, **fold** the page **under and up** along the lines.
4. Draw an **X** through the number by your name above and give this sheet to another member.
5. The **last** student gives this sheet to the teacher.

$1 = A lot$ $2 = Some$ $3 = A little$ $4 = Not at all$

_____ 1. We used words and pictures from the book to tell about our ideas.

_____ 2. Everyone had a fair chance to share and discuss.

_____ 3. We used our time to talk about the book—not other topics that didn't fit the book.

_____ 4. Our discussion helped me like and/or better understand the book.

- -

_____ 1. We used words and pictures from the book to tell about our ideas.

_____ 2. Everyone had a fair chance to share and discuss.

_____ 3. We used our time to talk about the book—not other topics that didn't fit the book.

_____ 4. Our discussion helped me like and/or better understand the book.

- -

_____ 1. We used words and pictures from the book to tell about our ideas.

_____ 2. Everyone had a fair chance to share and discuss.

_____ 3. We used our time to talk about the book—not other topics that didn't fit the book.

_____ 4. Our discussion helped me like and/or better understand the book.

- -

_____ 1. We used words and pictures from the book to tell about our ideas.

_____ 2. Everyone had a fair chance to share and discuss.

_____ 3. We used our time to talk about the book—not other topics that didn't fit the book.

_____ 4. Our discussion helped me like and/or better understand the book.

- -

Alike but Different
Multicultural Cinderella Stories

Teacher Tip

Helping students learn about different customs and cultures can be exciting and rewarding. One way to help students develop a better understanding of other cultures is to compare and contrast the same story told from different cultural viewpoints.

Procedure 3 can work well with this text set. As a starting point, you may want to read Marcia Brown's or Amy Ehrlich's versions of *Cinderella* as your core book because they represent the traditional European version which many of your students may be familiar with.

Text Set

Cendrillon: A Caribbean Cinderella
Robert D. San Souci
Simon & Schuster, 1998

The Turkey Girl: A Zuni Cinderella Story
Penny Pollock
Little, Brown, 1996

Cinderella
Retold by Amy Ehrlich (Charles Perrault)
Dial, 1985

Cinderella
Marcia Brown
Scribner, 1954

Sootface: An Ojibwa Cinderella Story
Robert D. San Souci
Delacorte Press, 1994

The Way Meat Loves Salt: A Cinderella Tale from the Jewish Tradition
Nina Jaffe
Henry Holt, 1998

Angkat: The Cambodian Cinderella
Jewell Reinhart Coburn
Shen's Books, 1998

The Korean Cinderella
Shirley Climo
HarperCollins, 1993

The Egyptian Cinderella
Shirley Climo
Thomas Y. Crowell, 1989

Cinder Edna
Ellen Jackson
Lothrop & Lee, 1994

Cinder-Elly
Frances Minters
Viking, 1994

Ashpet: An Appalachian Tale
Joanne Compton
Holiday House, 1994

CINDERELLA STORIES

Name _____

Write or draw your response to the Cinderella stories you read. Tell how the stories are alike and different.

Alike	Different

Write questions to ask or ideas to tell your group. Also write the page or a picture reminder.

Questions—Ideas   Page-Picture Reminder

1. _____

2. _____

3. _____

4. _____

Bilingual Bookmarks
Stories with Embedded Non-English Words and Expressions

Teacher Tip

Helping students on the road to language learning can take an interesting turn when students become familiar with non-English words and expressions from other countries or cultures. These non-English words and expressions, which are embedded in the text, can serve as springboards for student discussions not only about other countries and cultures but also about how students determined the meaning of the unfamiliar words or expressions.

Procedure 1 can work well with this text set. It's especially important to model for students how to use the Bilingual Bookmark so they can prepare it prior to their discussion.

Text Set

Gracias, Rosa
>   Michelle Markel
>   Albert Whitman & Co., 1995

Honk!
>   Pamela Duncan Edwards
>   Hyperion, 1998

Kitaq Goes Ice Fishing
>   Margaret Nicolai
>   Alaska Northwest Books, 1998

Chibi: A True Story from Japan
>   Barbara Brenner and Julia Takaya
>   Clarion Books, 1996

Ogbo: Sharing Life in an African Village
>   Ifeoma Onyefulu
>   Gulliver Books, 1996

Punia and the King of Sharks: A Hawaiian Folktale
>   Lee Wardlaw
>   Dial Books, 1997

My Horse of the North
>   Bruce McMillan
>   Scholastic, 1997

The Old Man and His Door
>   Gary Soto
>   Putnam's Sons, 1996

Fiesta Fireworks
>   George Ancona
>   Lothrop & Lee, 1998

Tapenum's Day
>   Kate Waters
>   Scholastic, 1996

Ali, Child of the Desert
>   Jonathan London
>   Lothrop & Lee, 1997

Bonjour, Lonnie
>   Faith Ringgold
>   Hyperion Books, 1996

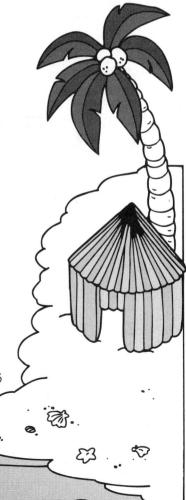

BILINGUAL BOOKMARKS

Name _____

Write and draw the non-English words and expressions from your book that you think are the most interesting.

Non-English Word or Expression	English Definition	Illustration or Example
_____	_____	_____
_____	_____	_____
_____	_____	_____
_____	_____	_____

Write questions to ask or ideas to tell your group. Also write the page or a picture reminder.

Questions—Ideas   Page-Picture Reminder

1. _____

2. _____

3. _____

4. _____

The Qualities of Critters
Books That Humorously Present the Characteristics of Different Animals

Teacher Tip

Helping students learn about and discuss the simple characteristics of different animals can sometimes be difficult if not downright dull. However, a fun way for students to learn about animals is to recognize what certain animals can and cannot do. The books in the following text set are sure to get your students talking about animals and, hopefully, heading for the nonfiction animal books in the library in order to read more.

Procedure 1 can work well with this text set. Since this literature circle may encourage your students to read more about animals, you may want to include this literature circle as part of a larger unit on animals.

Text Set

A Polar Bear Can Swim
> Harriet Ziefert
> Viking, 1998

Animals Should Definitely Not Act Like People
> Judi Barrett
> Atheneum, 1980

Guinea Pigs Don't Read Books
> Colleen Stanley Bare
> Dodd, Mead & Co., 1985

Mice Squeak, We Speak
> Arnold Shapiro
> G.P. Putnam's Sons, 1997

Please Don't Squeeze Your Boa, Noah!
> Marilyn Singer
> Henry Holt, 1995

Do Pigs Have Stripes?
> Melanie Walsh
> Houghton MIfflin, 1996

Dogs Don't Wear Sneakers
> Laura Numeroff
> Simon & Schuster, 1993

Who Hops?
> Katie Davis
> Harcourt Brace, 1998

Do Monkeys Tweet?
> Melanie Walsh
> Houghton Mifflin, 1997

Duck, Duck, Goose?
> Katya Arnold
> Holiday House, 1997

Smile if You're Human
> Neal Layton
> Dial Books, 1999

Chimps Don't Wear Glasses
> Laura Numeroff
> Simon & Schuster, 1995

CRITTERS

Name _____

Write and draw your response to the animal book you read. Be silly or serious!

Can and Cannot

A _____ can _____,

but a _____ cannot_____.

Draw What Your Animal Can Do	Draw What Your Animal Cannot Do

Write questions to ask or ideas to tell your group. Also write the page or a picture reminder.

Questions–Ideas   Page-Picture Reminder

1. _____

2. _____

3. _____

4. _____

BIOGRAPHIES
PEOPLE PORTRAITS OF FAMOUS PEOPLE

Teacher Tip

Helping students learn more about people who have had to overcome obstacles in order to achieve their chosen goals is one way of introducing students to positive role models. In addition, students can also learn from reading about people whose accomplishments were not recognized during their lifetimes and who died as "failures."

Procedure 1 can work well with this text set. You may want to choose one of the books listed as your core read-aloud book or choose from one of the many biography series such as Holiday House's *A Picture Book of . . .* or Bridgestone Books' *Photo-Illustrated Biographies*.

Text Set

Sacagawea: The Journey to the West
Elaine Raphael and Don Bolognese
Scholastic, 1994

Bill Pickett: Rodeo Riding Cowboy
Andrea Pinkney
Harcourt Brace, 1996

Mother Teresa: Saint of the Poor
Nina Morgan
Raintree/Steck-Vaughn, 1998

Count Me In (Note: This is an autobiography.)
Cal Ripkin, Jr. with Greg Brown
Taylor Publishing, 1995

**Stone Girl, Bone Girl: The Story of
Mary Anning Laurence**
Laurence Anholt and Sheila Moxley
Orchard, 1999

A Boy Called Slow: The True Story of Sitting Bull
Joseph Bruchac
Philomel Books, 1994

**Purple Mountain Majesties: The Story of
Katharine Lee Bates and "America the Beautiful"**
Barbara Younger
Dutton Children's Books, 1998

Where Lincoln Walked
Raymond Bial
Walker & Co., 1998

Eleanor
Barbara Cooney
Viking, 1996

Ida B. Wells-Barnett
Patricia McKissack
Enslow Publishers, 1991

El Chino
Allen Say
Houghton Mifflin, 1990

Snowflake Bentley
Jacqueline Briggs Martin
Houghton Mifflin, 1998

BIOGRAPHIES

Name _____

Write or draw your response to the biography stories you read. Each box below can be either a picture frame for your drawing, a book page for your words or one of each.

The Most Important or Brave Thing This Person Did	This Person's Most Important Talent or Ability

Write questions to ask or ideas to tell your group. Also write the page or a picture reminder.

Questions—Ideas   Page-Picture Reminder

1. _____

2. _____

3. _____

4. _____

SEEKING SOLUTIONS
STORIES IN WHICH CHARACTERS SOLVE A PROBLEM

Teacher Tip

A character in search of a solution to his or her problem is often the basic plot of many stories. The character's problem is often the source of the story's conflict while the character's different attempts at problem solving move the plot forward.

Some of the stories in the text set below are stories about individuals solving problems while other stories focus on groups working together to solve a problem. You may want to consider reading one of each type of story as your core books before implementing Procedure 1 or 3.

Text Set

Nine for California
> Sonia Levitin
> Orchard Books, 1996

What! Cried Granny: An Almost Bedtime Story
> Kate Lum
> Dial Books, 1999

Lon PoPo: A Red-Riding Hood Story from China
> Ed Young
> Philomel, 1989

Horace and Morris but Mostly Delores
> James Howe
> Atheneum, 1999

Mouse Practice
> Emily Arnold McCully
> Scholastic, 1999

The Hatseller and the Monkeys: A West African Folktale
> Baba Wague Dlakite
> Scholastic, 1999

What Newt Could Do for Turtle
> Jonathan London
> Candlewick Press, 1996

Mrs. Toggle's Zipper
> Robin Pulver
> Four Winds, 1990

Owen
> Kevin Henkes
> Greenwillow, 1993

The Enormous Carrot
> Vladimir Vagin
> Scholastic, 1998

Tortoise Solves a Problem
> Avner Katz
> HarperCollins, 1993

The Chicken Salad Club
> Marsha Diane Arnold
> Dial, 1998

Problem Solving

Name _____

Write or draw what you think the main character's problem was and how she or he solved the problem.

Problem	Solution

Write questions to ask or ideas to tell your group. Also write the page or a picture reminder.

Questions—Ideas   Page-Picture Reminder

1. _____

2. _____

3. _____

4. _____

Factual Fiction
Stories Based on Historical Facts

Teacher Tip

Reading historical fiction helps students realize and appreciate that history is filled with real-life people involved in real-life events. Often the people in the stories are just like the students themselves. Many of the people in the stories, however, had to respond with enormous courage to historical events. How each student would have responded in the same circumstance can be an excellent discussion topic.

It's important to explain to students that historical fiction is based on real people and real events but that the details of the action and conversations are fictitious unless a historically accurate direct quotation is used by the author. Procedure 1 can work well with this text.

Text Set

Boy of the Deeps
> Ian Wallace
> DK Publishing, 1999

An Outlaw Thanksgiving
> Emily Arnold McCully
> Dial Books, 1998

Black Cowboy, Wild Horses
> Julius Lester
> Dial Books, 1998

Passage to Freedom: The Sugihara Story
> Ken Mochizuki
> Lee & Low Books, 1997

Marven of the Great North Woods
> Kathryn Lasky
> Harcourt Brace, 1997

The Lion and the Unicorn
> Shirley Hughes
> DK Publishing, 1999

A Band of Angels: A Story Inspired by the Jubilee Singers
> Deborah Hopkinson
> Atheneum Books, 1999

Kate Shelley: Bound for Legend
> Robert D. San Souci
> Dial Books, 1995

So Far from the Sea
> Eve Bunting
> Clarion Books, 1998

Mr. Lincoln's Whiskers
> Karen B. Winnick
> Boyds Mills Press, 1996

Mailing May
> Michael O. Tunnell
> Greenwillow, 1997

The Lily Cupboard
> Shulamith Levey Oppenheim
> HarperCollins, 1992

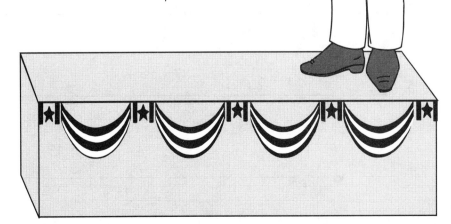

HISTORICAL FICTION

Name _____

Draw your favorite scene from the book so you can tell about it later during discussion.

Book Title: _____

[ ]

Write questions to ask or ideas to tell your group. Also write the page or a picture reminder.

Questions—Ideas   Page-Picture Reminder

1. _____

2. _____

3. _____

4. _____

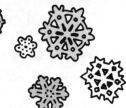

POETRY PLACE
POETRY BOOKS AND BOOKS WITH RHYTHM AND RHYMES

Teacher Tip

Poetry can provide a positive literacy experience for students who often struggle with longer pieces of literature. At the same time, poetry requires all students to use their imaginations and give their undivided attention to each and every word the poet uses.

You may want to use one of the books from the text set or any of Jack Prelutsky or Shel Silverstein's poems for your modeling session. There are several ways you can set up your literature circles. Each circle can read the same poem or each student can choose his or her favorite poem from the book or each student can choose a favorite poem by a specific poet.

Text Set

Winter Lullaby
Barbara Seuling
Browndeer Press, 1998

Kids Pick the Funniest Poems
Bruce Lansky
Simon & Schuster, 1991

A Pair of Red Sneakers
Lisa Lawston
Orchard Books, 1998

Hello Toes! Hello Feet!
Ann Whitford Paul
DK Publishing, 1998

Summer Legs
Anita Hakkinen
Henry Holt, 1995

The Bookworm's Feast: A Potluck of Poems
J. Patrick Lewis
Dial, 1999

Sports! Sports! Sports!
Lee Bennett Hopkins
HarperCollins, 1999

Good Rhymes, Good Times
Lee Bennett Hopkins
HarperCollins, 1995

Sometimes I Wonder if Poodles Like Noodles
Laura Numeroff and Tim Bowers
Simon & Schuster, 1999

Aska's Sea Creatures
Warabe Aska
Doubleday, 1994

Greetings, Sun
Phillis Gershator
DK Publishing, 1998

Cool Melons—Turn to Frogs! The Life and Poems of Issa
Matthew Gollub
Lee & Low Books, 1998

Extra Innings: Baseball Poems
Lee Bennett Hopkins
Harcourt Brace, 1993

Laugh-eteria
Douglas Florian
Harcourt Brace, 1999

Flower Garden
Eve Bunting
Harcourt Brace, 1994

There Was an Old Lady Who Swallowed a Trout!
Teri Sloat
Henry Holt, 1998

Insectlopedia
Douglas Florian
Harcourt Brace, 1998

Sun Sand Sea Sail
Nicki Weiss
Greenwillow, 1989

Very Best (Almost) Friends: Poems of Friendship
Paul B. Janeczko
Candlewick Press, 1999

POETRY

Name _____

In the space below, write one or two of your favorite lines from the poem you've chosen. Next, draw a picture that tells about the lines of poetry.

Title of Poem: _____

Name of Poet: _____

Favorite Lines   **Drawing**

_____

_____

_____

_____

_____

Write questions to ask or ideas to tell your group. Also write the poetry line reminder.

Questions—Ideas   Poetry Line Reminder

1. _____

2. _____

3. _____

4. _____

44

LETTERS FOR LEARNERS
ABC Books That Entertain and Teach

Teacher Tip

Alphabet books teach and entertain in a way no other type of book can. Built around a concept or "pattern" rather than a plot, alphabet books appeal to older as well as younger readers whose interests range from cute (*The Kern Alphabet Book*) to clever (*Tomorrow's Alphabet*).

Procedure 2 can work well with the text set below. Having each student share a different alphabet book will enable students to discuss each book's art and concept. (Concept refers to whether an author uses cowboys or apes in capes to illustrate his ABCs!) If your students are older, however, you may want to consider having them read two or three of the same alphabet books that are a bit more sophisticated. This allows students in each circle to discuss each book's unique approach to the alphabet as well as help students generate ideas for their own alphabet books.

Text Set

Everything to Spend the Night from A to Z
> Ann Whitford Paul
> DK Publishing, 1999

The Kern Alphabet Book
> Donna Kern
> Cove Press, 1998

The Disappearing Alphabet
> Richard Wilbur
> Harcourt Brace, 1997

The Hole by the Apple Tree: An A-Z Discovery Tale
> Nancy Polette
> Greenwillow Books, 1992

Q Is for Duck, an Alphabet Guessing Game
> Mary Elting and Michael Folsom
> Houghton Mifflin, 1980

The Cowboy ABC
> Chris Demarest
> DK Publishing, 1999

Ape in a Cape
> Fritz Eichenberg
> Harcourt Brace, 1952

Tomorrow's Alphabet
> George Shannon
> Greenwillow, 1996

The Z Was Zapped
> Chris Van Allsburg
> Houghton Mifflin, 1987

Amazon ABC
> Kathryn Darling
> Lothrop & Lee, 1996

A Yellowstone ABC
> Cyd Martin
> Roberts Rinehart, 1992

The Jet Alphabet Book
> Jerry Polatta
> Charlesbridge, 1999

ABC Books

Name _____

The alphabet book you read followed a pattern. Think of a pattern of your own and choose three alphabet letters to write about or draw pictures about.

Title of Your Mini Alphabet Book: _____

Write questions to ask or ideas to tell your group. Also write the page or a picture reminder.

Questions—Ideas   Page-Picture Reminder

1. _____

2. _____

3. _____

4. _____

Looking Closely at Books
Books That Contain Signs and Stories Told Through Pictures Only

Teacher Tip

"Being literate" is a very broad phrase that encompasses among other things the ability to read books as well as the ability to interpret information from pictures and diagrams. Students need "visual literacy" that enables them to "read" the world around them.

Procedure 1 or 2 can work well with the text set below. Younger students will enjoy the many books with signs in them like *Truck* and *I Walk and Read* while older students will enjoy picture-only books such as *Tuesday* and *The Grey Lady and the Strawberry Snatcher*. *Officer Buckle and Gloria* and *The Signmaker's Assistant* are good choices for the read-aloud core book because they emphasize the importance of reading and following the directions on signs.

Text Set

Alphabet City
Stephen T. Johnson
Viking, 1995

I Read Signs
Tana Hoban
Greenwillow Books, 1983

The Grey Lady and the Strawberry Snatcher
Molly Bang
Four Winds Press, 1980

Officer Buckle and Gloria
Peggy Rathmann
G.P. Putnam's Sons, 1995

Harriet Reads Signs and More Signs
Betsy and Giulio Maestro
Crown Publishers, 1981

Reading
Richard Allington and Kathleen Krall
Raintree, 1980

I Walk and Read
Tana Hoban
Greenwillow Books, 1983

Truck
Donald Crews
Mulberry Books, 1980

Tuesday
David Wiesner
Clarion Books, 1991

Follow Carl!
Alexandra Day
Farrar Straus Giroux, 1998

Tabby: A Story in Pictures
Aliki
HarperCollins, 1995

The Signmaker's Assistant
Tedd Arnold
Dial, 1992

LOOKING CLOSELY AT BOOKS

Name _____

The book you've just read either contained signs or told a story with
pictures only or perhaps your teacher asked you to read one of each. If your book contained
signs, complete Response A. If your book told a story with pictures only, complete Response B.

Response A

Draw two signs you think are important.	Draw two silly signs for school or home.

Response B

Tell the story's beginning.	Tell the story's middle.	Tell the story's ending.

Write questions to ask or ideas to tell your group. Also write the page or a picture reminder.

Questions—Ideas   Page-Picture Reminder

1. _____

2. _____

3. _____

4. _____

NIFTY NUMBERS
BOOKS THAT CONTAIN MATH CONCEPTS

Teacher Tip

There are many delightful books students can read that not only will help them understand different math concepts but also engage them in entertaining stories as well. Having fun with the math woven into the stories just may make math time and literature circle time two of your students' favorite times of the day! In addition to the books listed below, HarperCollins publishes a Math Start series and Simon & Schuster publishes The Pig Family math concept series.

Procedure 1 can work well with this text set. If your students are younger, however, you may want each student to read a different counting book and share it with the group members. For their responses, students can follow the book's pattern and add five numbers to the author's total.

Text Set

Math Curse
> Jon Scieszka
> Viking, 1995

Jump, Kangaroo, Jump!
> Stuart Murphy
> HarperCollins, 1999

12 Ways to Get to 11
> Eve Merriam
> Simon & Schuster, 1993

Cook-a-Doodle-Doo!
> Janet Stevens
> Harcourt Brace, 1999

One Duck Stuck
> Phyllis Root
> Candlewick Press, 1998

Sir Cumference and the First Round Table
> Cindy Neuschwander
> Charlesbridge, 1997

The Doorbell Rang
> Pat Hutchins
> Greenwillow, 1986

Counting Crocodiles
> Judy Sierra
> Harcourt Brace, 1997

Bunny Money
> Rosemary Wells
> Dial, 1997

Measuring Penny
> Loreen Leedy
> Henry Holt, 1997

In Window Eight, the Moon Is Late
> Diane Worfolk Allison
> Little Brown, 1988

One Grain of Rice: A Mathematical Folktale
> Demi
> Scholastic, 1997

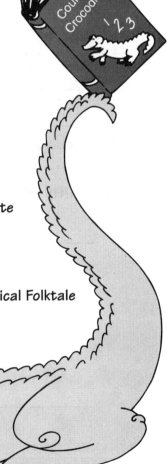

NIFTY NUMBERS

Name _____

The story you read had math woven into it. Perhaps the main character added, subtracted or measured something. To help your group begin discussing the book's math ideas, write a story problem to share with your group. The problem should use the same kind of math used in your book and include the main character.

Title: _____

Story Problem

_____

_____

_____

_____

_____

Answer

_____

_____

_____

_____

_____

Write questions to ask or ideas to tell your group. Also write the page or a picture reminder.

Questions—Ideas   ## Page-Picture Reminder

1. _____

2. _____

3. _____

4. _____

PICTURE PERFECT
BOOKS THAT ILLUSTRATE THE ART OF AND IN STORYTELLING

Teacher Tip

An outstanding children's picture book is one whose illustrations and text are so harmoniously woven together that the reader not only experiences the story through the text but also through the illustrations. Since children learn to "picture read" before they learn to read text fluently, literature circles can provide students with a wonderful opportunity to discuss different kinds of picture book art.

Procedure 1, 2 or 3 can work with this type of literature circle. However, you may want to use a different type of introduction by first reading one of the books where the main character is an artist. (*Incredible Ned* is excellent!) Many of your students may be able to relate to the characters in these books because they, like the characters, have strong artistic talents, too.

Next, share excerpts from books in the second text set so students have an opportunity to "meet" various illustrators and learn what inspires them. Finally, introduce various books illustrated by the artist listed or let students choose from the Caldecott winner and honor book list.

Text Set

Books in Which the Main Character Is an Artist

Incredible Ned
  Bill Maynard
  G.P. Putnam, 1997

Harold and the Purple Crayon
  Crockett Johnson
  Harper & Row, 1955

Annie's Gifts
  Angela Medearis
  Just Us Books, 1994

Books That Introduce Various Artists and Illustrators

A Caldecott Celebration: Six Artists and Their Paths to the Caldecott Medal
  Leonard S. Marcus
  Walker & Co., 1998

Meet the Authors and Illustrators
  Deborah Kovacs and
  James Preller
  Scholastic, 1994

Talking with Artists (Volumes I, II and III)
  Pat Cummings
  Simon & Schuster,
  1992 and 1995

Recommended Illustrators

Brian Pinkney
Molly Bang
Janet Stevens
David Wisniewski

Trina Schart Hyman
David Wiesner
Peter Catalanotto
Steven Kellogg

John Steptoe
Chris Van Allsburg
David Shannon
Allen Say

The Caldecott winner and honor book list can be accessed at the following addresses:

http://www.ala.org/alsc/caldecott.html
http://ils.unc.edu/award/chome.html

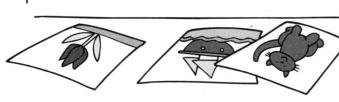

Picture Book Art

Name _____

What makes a picture book special? It's the pictures, of course! Sometimes pictures or illustrations, as they are called, can make a scary story even scarier and a funny story even funnier! Pictures also help you understand a story because they tell the story in drawings.

Tell what you liked and didn't like about the pictures in your books. Your teacher will tell you if you should read two books illustrated by the same artist or two books illustrated by two different artists.

Title: _____ Illustrator: _____

Liked a lot   Liked Somewhat   Didn't Like

Title: _____ Illustrator: _____

Liked a lot   Liked Somewhat   Didn't Like

Write questions to ask or ideas to tell your group. Also write the page or a picture reminder.

Questions—Ideas   ## Page-Picture Reminder

1. _____

2. _____

3. _____

4. _____

FRACTURED FAIRY TALES
BOOKS THAT TELL TALES WITH A TWIST

Teacher Tip

Retelling familiar fairy tales in a unique, unexpected way has become very popular in recent years. These tales often achieve their "twist" by changing the original tale's characters, setting and ending.

Procedure 1 can work well with this text set. You may want to read aloud several of the original tales if you think students are unfamiliar with them.

Text Set

Gordon Loggins and the Three Bears
    Linda Bailey
    Kids Can, 1997

The Prog Frince: A Mixed-Up Tale
    C. Drew Lamm
    Orchard Books, 1999

The Fourth Little Pig
    Teresa Celsi
    Raintree/Steck-Vaughn, 1990

The True Story of the 3 Little Pigs!
    Jon Scieszka and Lane Smith
    Viking, 1989

Bubba the Cowboy Prince: A Fractured Texas Tale
    Helen Ketterman
    Scholastic, 1997

The Stinky Cheese Man and Other Fairly Stupid Tales
    Jon Scieszka and Lane Smith
    Viking, 1992

The Principal's New Clothes
    Stephanie Calmenson
    Scholastic, 1989

Rumpelstiltskin's Daughter
    Diane Stanley
    Morrow Junior Books, 1997

The Bootmaker and the Elves
    Susan Lowell
    Orchard Books, 1997

Sleeping Ugly
    Jane Yolen
    Putnam, 1981

The Frog Prince Continued
    Jon Scieszka
    Puffin, 1994

Somebody and the Three Blairs
    Marilyn Tolhurst
    Orchard, 1991

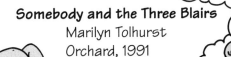

Fractured Fairy Tales

Name _____

To make old stories new again, authors often change a story's characters, setting and ending. Be an author and tell how you'd change your story's characters, setting and ending to make a new story. (The word *setting* means "where the story takes place.")

Characters

_____

_____

_____

Setting

_____

_____

_____

Ending

_____

_____

_____

Write questions to ask or ideas to tell your group. Also write the page or a picture reminder.

Questions—Ideas   Page-Picture Reminder

1. _____

2. _____

3. _____

4. _____

READING REALLY MATTERS
STORIES THAT ILLUSTRATE THE JOY OF READING

Teacher Tip

Helping students to enjoy reading—not just learning how to read—is an important educational goal. A student who knows how to read and enjoys doing it will become a lifelong reader.

This is the only text set listed in this book where the teacher must read a specific title as the core read-aloud book. George Ella Lyon's *Book* (DK Publishing, 1999) will certainly be a book you will want to add to your classroom library. After reading *Book* aloud, you may want to have students complete the response portion of their literature circle sheet and then introduce the other books in the text set.

Procedure 1 can work well with this text set that emphasizes the joy of reading. You may also want to follow up this text set with poems from Lee Bennett Hopkins' book, *Good Books, Good Times* (HarperCollins, 1990).

Text Set

The Day of Ahmed's Secret
Florence Parry Heide
Lothrop & Lee, 1990

Read for Me, Mama
Vashanti Rahaman
Boyds Mills, 1997

Richard Wright and the Library Card
William Miller
Lee & Low Books, 1997

My Great Aunt Arizona
Gloria Houston
HarperCollins, 1992

I Hate to Read
Rita Marshall
Creative Company, 1993

Just Open a Book
P.K. Hallinan
Ideals Children's Books, 1995

Tomas and the Library Lady
Pat Mora
Knopf, 1997

Wolf!
Becky Bloom
Orchard Books, 1999

Wednesday Surprise
Eve Bunting
Clarion, 1989

Oh, How I Wished I Could Read!
John Gile
Worzalla, 1995

Thank You, Mr. Falker
Patricia Polacco
Philomel, 1998

Clara and the Bookwagon
Carolyn Croll
HarperCollins, 1988

Reading Really Matters

Name _____

The book your teacher read aloud to you talked about books being like fields of words, treasure chests and houses with windows and doors. What do you think books are like?

> A book is a ship that can sail you away,
> Anytime you want, anytime of day.
>
> A book is a roller coaster going up and down.
> Some make me laugh. Some make me frown.

Write or draw what you think books are like.

```


```

Write questions to ask or ideas to tell your group. Also write the page or a picture reminder.

Questions—Ideas   Page-Picture Reminder

1. _____

2. _____

3. _____

4. _____

SENSATIONAL SERIES
BOOK SERIES TOO GOOD TO MISS!

Teacher Tip

Book series are great for getting students excited about reading and going back for more. Most series center on notable characters whose adventures or misadventures keep students turning the pages until they've reached the end and ask, "Got any more?"

Introduce students to a number of different series before implementing Procedure 1 or 4. In addition to series by authors, HarperCollins publishes the I Can Read Book and Little House Chapter Books series, Random House publishes its Step into Reading series, and DK Publishing's Eyewitness Readers is an excellent nonfiction series.

Text Set

David Adler
    Cam Jansen
    Viking

Barbara Park
    Junie B. Jones
    Random House

Arnold Lobel
    Frog and Toad
    Harper & Row

Paula Danzinger
    Amber Brown
    Putnam

Betsy Byars
    The Golly Sisters
    HarperTrophy

Judy Delton
    Pee Wee Scouts
    Bantam

Barbara Joosee
    Wild Willie
    Clarion

Jamie Gilson
    Itchy Richard
    Clarion Books

Marjorie Sharmat
    Nate the Great
    Coward-McCann

Louis Sachar
    Marvin Redpost
    Random House

James Preller
    Jigsaw Jones
    Scholastic

Suzy Kline
    Horrible Harry
    Puffin

Jon Scieszka
    Time Warp Trio
    Puffin

Nancy Shaw/Margot Apple
    Sheep
    Houghton Mifflin

Peggy Parish
    Amelia Bedelia
    Harper & Row

Cynthia Rylant
    Mr. Putter and Tabby
    Harcourt Brace

    Henry and Mudge
    Bradbury Press
    Simon & Schuster

    Poppleton
    Scholastic

    Cobblestreet Cousins
    Simon & Schuster

Name _____

CHARACTER SKETCHER

Your role as the Character Sketcher is to help your group members better understand the main characters in your book. Think about what the characters think, say and do. These thoughts, words and actions will tell you what the characters are like. Use describing words like *brave* and *kind* in the left-hand column. In the right-hand column, use examples from your book to support your ideas.

Character's Name: _____

What This Character Is Like	**Examples from the Book** (page __)
1. _____	_____
2. _____	_____
3. _____	_____
4. _____	_____

Character's Name: _____

What This Character Is Like	**Examples from the Book** (page __)
1. _____	_____
2. _____	_____
3. _____	_____
4. _____	_____

SCENE SETTER

When you read, the author's words help your imagination create a picture in your mind of the story's setting (where the story takes place) or a special action that takes place in the story. Your role as the Scene Setter is to share your imagination with your group members by selecting three different scenes from your book and drawing one of the scenes in the space provided. After each scene, list three words that describe the scene.

Scene 1: _____ Page(s) _____

Three descriptive words: _____ _____ _____

Scene 2: _____ Page(s) _____

Three descriptive words: _____ _____ _____

Scene 3: _____ Page(s) _____

Three descriptive words: _____ _____ _____

I chose to illustrate the above scene because _____

_____

Name _____

DIALOGUE DESCRIBER

Authors use dialogue (the words that characters say) to help readers understand each of the story's characters and how they get along or don't get along with one another. Dialogue can tell a reader if a character is angry, sad or happy with himself and those around him. Your role as the Dialogue Describer is to help your group discuss different examples of dialogue in the story and their importance.

Dialogue said by _____ Page(s) _____

Dialogue Example: _____

_____

This dialogue is important because _____

_____

Dialogue said by _____ Page(s) _____

Dialogue Example: _____

_____

This dialogue is important because _____

_____

Dialogue said by _____ Page(s) _____

Dialogue Example: _____

_____

This dialogue is important because _____

_____

Name _____

HAVE-IN-COMMON CONNECTOR

Many times readers understand how a character feels because they've had the same kinds of feelings or have had something similar happen to them. Your role as the Have-in-Common Connector is to help your group discover what they "have in common" with the characters and events in your book. Complete the left-hand column and the bottom portion of this role sheet before meeting with your group. During discussion, complete the right-hand column.

I Have These Things in Common with the Book's Character(s)	Group Has These Things in Common with the Book's Character(s)

Tell how this book is like other books you've read. Give titles, authors and examples.

Title: _____ Author: _____

Examples: _____

_____

Title: _____ Author: _____

Examples: _____

_____

Title: _____ Author: _____

Examples: _____

_____

Name _____

PLOT PERSON

A story has a beginning, a middle and an ending. The events that make up this beginning, middle and ending are called the plot line or plot of the story. Your role as the Plot Person is to help your group members understand and agree about the events in the story. The Plot Chart* below will help you.

The character or characters in the story are the **Somebody**. The Somebody **Wanted** something in the story. **But** there was a problem that got in the way or stopped the Somebody from getting what she wanted. **So** the character or characters had to solve the problem.

Plot Chart: The Three Little Pigs
Somebody: The three little pigs
Wanted: To build homes of their own and live happily ever after
But: The big bad wolf wanted to eat the three little pigs
So: The three little pigs tricked the wolf and lived happily ever after

Somebody: _____

_____

Wanted: _____

_____

But: _____

_____

So: _____

_____

*Originally developed by Dr. Barbara Schmidt of California State University-Sacramento.

WORDSMITH

Authors work hard to use just the right words when writing their stories. As a reader, you know that authors use special and sometimes unfamiliar words to describe a setting or an action. For example, a story that takes place in a "glen" takes place in a valley because the word *valley* describes or defines the word *glen*. Your role as the Wordsmith is to help your group members discuss important, unfamiliar or unusual words from the story. As you read your book, you may want to put sticky notes on pages where you find words you'd like to discuss.

Word: _____ Page(s): _____ The word is used in the sentence below:

_____

As it's used in the sentence above, this word means _____

Two other words that are like this word are _____ _____

Word: _____ Page(s): _____ The word is used in the sentence below:

_____

As it's used in the sentence above, this word means _____

Two other words that are like this word are _____ _____

Word: _____ Page(s): _____ The word is used in the sentence below:

_____

As it's used in the sentence above, this word means _____

Two other words that are like this word are _____ _____

Word: _____ Page(s): _____ The word is used in the sentence below:

_____

As it's used in the sentence above, this word means _____

Two other words that are like this word are _____ _____

DECISION DIRECTOR

In every fiction book, characters make decisions that move the story forward to its conclusion. Your role as the Decision Director is to help your group members look more closely at the important decisions the main character(s) made and how the decisions moved the story to its conclusion. Each decision can be broken down into three parts: Conflict, Decision, Results.

Conflict	Decision	Results
Main character finds beaten dog. Knows the owner.	Main character decides to help the dog.	Main character hides dog without telling parents.

Opening Conflict	Decision	Results

Next Conflict	Decision	Results

Next Conflict	Decision	Conclusion